CAT SHAMING

PEDRO ANDRADE

Andrews McMeel Publishing®

a division of Andrews McMeel Universal

FOREWORD

When I started my *Dog Shaming* blog in 2012, I had no idea the phenomenon it would become. What began as an innocent, humorous post, born of frustration—we had photographed our male wiener dog, Beau, after he'd just ingested a good chunk of my then-fiancé's underwear with the sign "I am an underwear eating jerk!" and posted it to my blog—quickly turned into an Internet sensation.

Turns out that dog owners were not the only ones in need of an avenue to vent their frustration; other memes have followed suit, and none so fitting as Pedro Andrade's *Cat Shaming*. Cat owners everywhere will commune over the antics photographed within, with which they are all too familiar. Cats who prefer the space just outside the litter box to do their business. Kitties who whine and cry into the wee hours, sleeping on their owners' heads or waking them at 4 a.m., only to spend their daytime hours napping undisturbed while their owners sleepwalk through the daily grind. Felines who cause broken bones and show no remorse. These are just a few of the pet antics that most of us know and love—well, maybe we don't *love* the antics themselves, but we certainly do adore the furry best friends who cause the mischief.

Venting is often the best medicine. Like the many dog-lovers who still send me photos of their pets misbehaving, cat-lovers everywhere will enjoy the same commiseration—and fun!—now that shaming is not just for dogs.

Enjoy the catharsis.

Woof,
Pascale Lemire
Dogshaming.com

I was a lovely tiny kitty a year ago. Now all grown up, I still hang out in the same plant, messing up the place!

I poop in
the bathtub

Equally mean and cute.
Enjoys biting, preferably
flesh

I ATE MY OWNER'S DESSERT
WHILE SHE WAS TAKING A
CAT-SHAMING PHOTO OF THE
OTHER CAT.

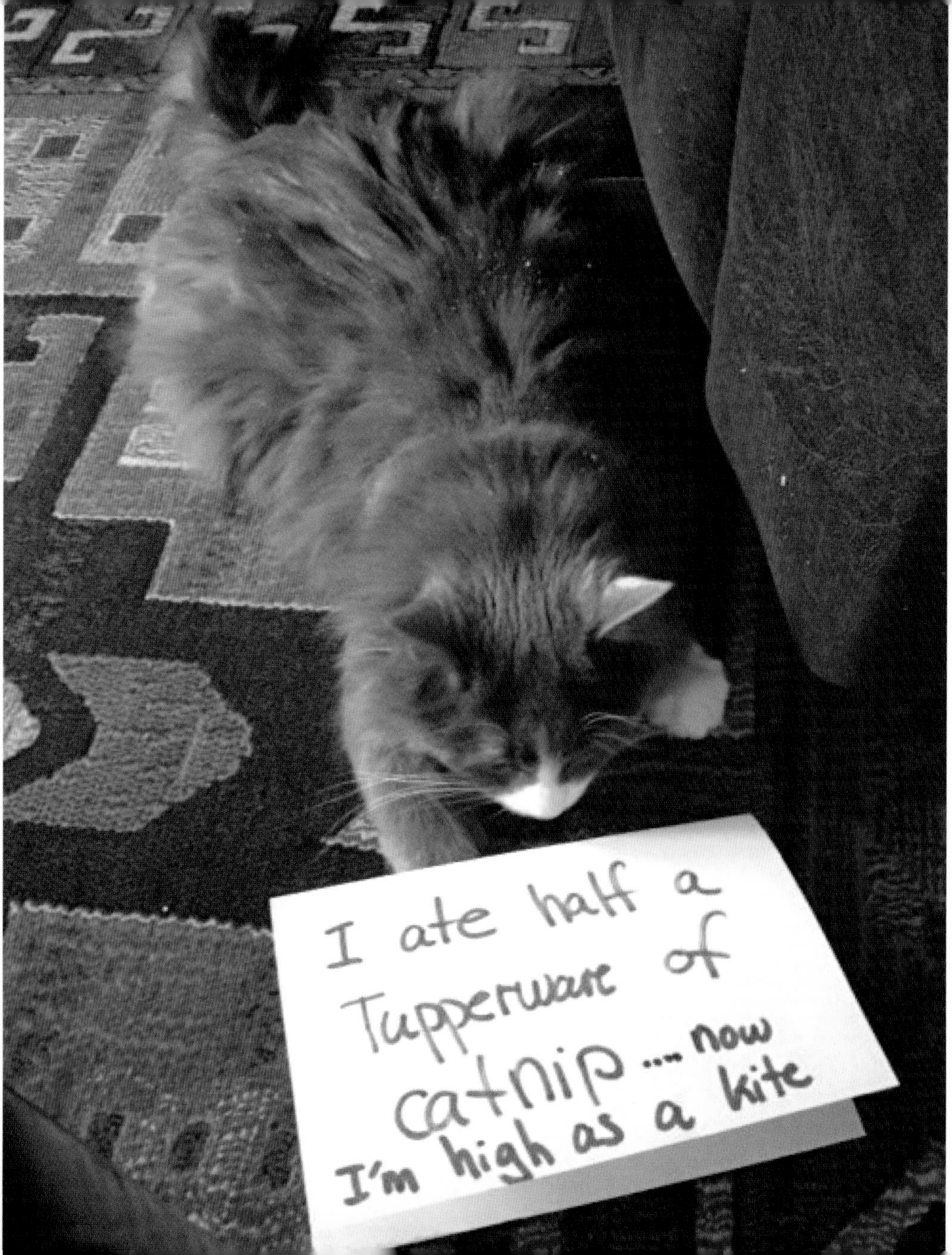
I ate half a
Tupperware of
catnip .... now
I'm high as a kite

I EAT FOOD
SO FAST THAT I
THROW IT UP INTO MY
BOWL... AND THEN I
JUST KEEP ON EATING

I love to beg for food at 5 A.M. even though my plate is full.
-Scarr

I LEFT THIS CHAIR ALONE FOR ABOUT 5 YEARS UNTIL MOMMY STARTED LOOKING AT THIS WEBSITE CALLED "DOG SHAMING" AND LAUGHING ABOUT HOW FUNNY IT WAS, SO I DECIDED TO SHOW HER THAT CATS CAN BE FUNNY, TOO!

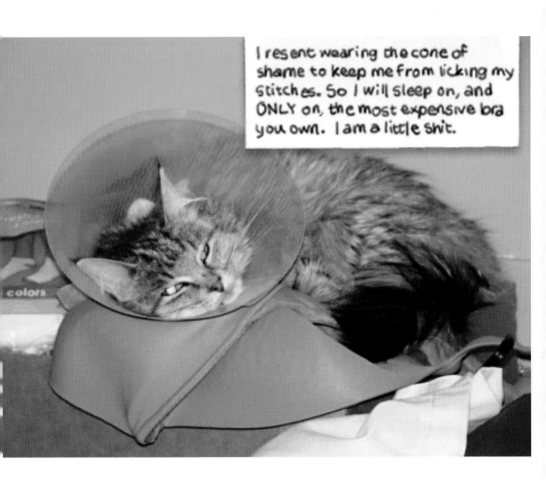

"I've pooped in the bathtub every day for 11 years. Only my resemblance to Winnie the Pooh keeps me out of the dog house."

36

I ate 2 feet of ribbon. Mom had to pull the poopy ribbon out of my butt at 4:00 this morning. I'd do it again, given the chance.

My food has to be spread out all over the floor like "chicken feed," or else I'll eat it too fast and puke it up.

And then I'll eat it again.

I HAVE LOST LESS THAN ONE POUND ON MY 10-YEAR-LONG DIET.

I'm Ellie...
this morning I
Stole my mom's
bacon crunch wrap
And, I have NO
remorse!!

I HUNT, KILL & EAT RABBITS WHOLE. AFTER OBTAINING ALL THEIR FLEAS I RETURN HOME & PUKE BLOOD, BONES, FUR & GUTS ALL OVER THE CARPET. I ALSO STEAL SOY MILK BOXES AND CORN COBS.

MUCH LOVE, JUDE.

I shred your papertowel during dinner so you can't wipe your hands

I pissed
on my mom's
UGG BOOT!
BAD KITTY

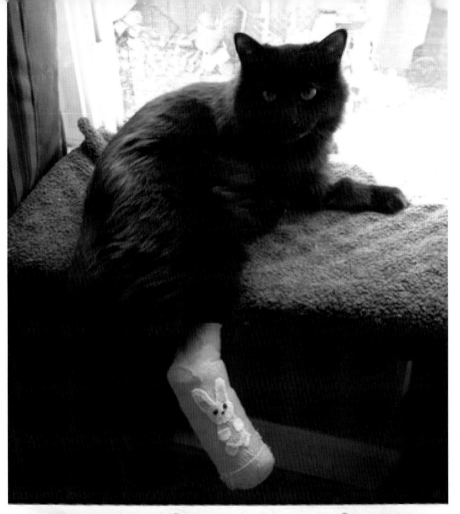

I moonlight as a Cirque du Soleil performer. My acrobatics cost me a broken toe, a splint for 6 1/2 weeks, and my mom $4,000.
I love you, Mommy! -XOXO, Arya, the Acrobat
P.S. When can I start performing again?

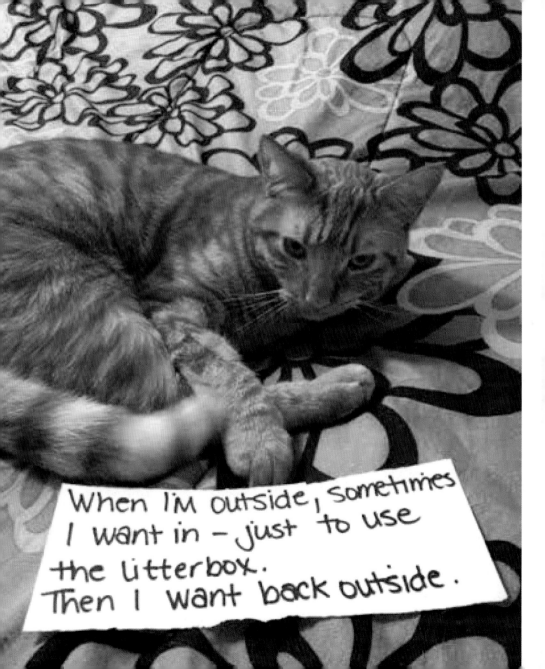

I PULL BOOKS OUT OF BOOKSHELVES AND SHRED THEM.

I'M SMUG AND UNREPENTANT.

Hello..... MY NAME IS LOKI OXFORD.
MY PARENTS SAY I HAVE A "BLANKET FETISH",
PERSONALLY.... THE BLANKETS ARE MY
SEX SLAVES!

I LIKE TO ATTACK THE SMALL DACHSHUND,
THE BIG PITBULL, AND THE OLD BLIND TERRIER,
··· I DO NOT DISCRIMINATE! ☹

I ATE MY HUMAN'S IGUANA'S TAIL... CLEAN OFF!
DIRTY HAMPERS ARE MY HAVEN!!
WHEN I'M ALONE WITH MY HUMAN, I'M AN
ANGEL. BUT WHEN THE DOGS ARE AROUND...
··· I'M AN A$$HOLE!

LOKI

I've eaten plant fertilizer,
an entire corn on the cob,
and a new pair of sandals
in the last 48 hours.

Shame level: 0

Oh, you're home! :)
BTW, Someone threw
up on the carpet...
Don't worry. I ate it.
xoxo —Chessa :)

My name is Sasha. I refuse to walk on the floor so I have taken to digging in the couch and peeing on my dad's pillows. I am an asshole.

I PEED ON MY MOM'S
LEGS WHILE SHE SLEPT.
SHE YELLED @ ME +
CHANGED ALL THE LINEN
SO I DECIDED TO
DIARRHEA ON THE END
OF THE BED THEN GET
UP @ 4AM TO SING...

I chewed my
mom's Apple
computer cord and
she had to pay
$119 to replace it!

I pooped ALL
over the house AND
rolled in it.

I SIT IN THIS BOX
AND SUCK UP ALL OF
THE HEAT LIKE IT IS MY
OWN PERSONAL SAUNA!

I'm Colbie, and I'm addicted to treats! I figured out how to open up the cabinets in the kitchen, and now I open the one under the drawer where they keep the treats, push it open from the inside, and climb in!

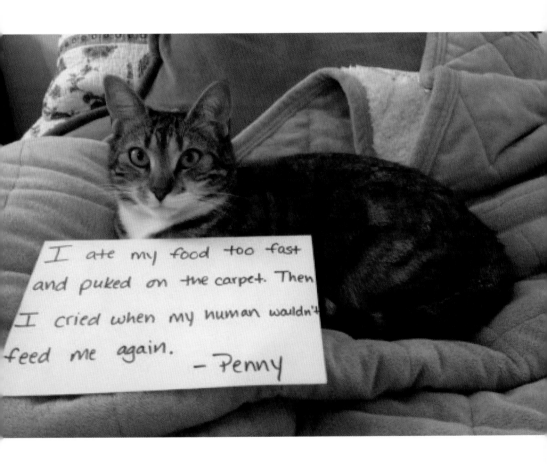

I ate my food too fast and puked on the carpet. Then I cried when my human wouldn't feed me again. — Penny

I am so proud of my poop that when Mom & Dad are sleeping I make sure they can smell it by sticking my butt in their faces!

♡ Alex

I ripped the
toilet paper in
the bathroom to
shreds. Twice.

I stalk the canary. He looks yummy but 'they' won't let me eat him.

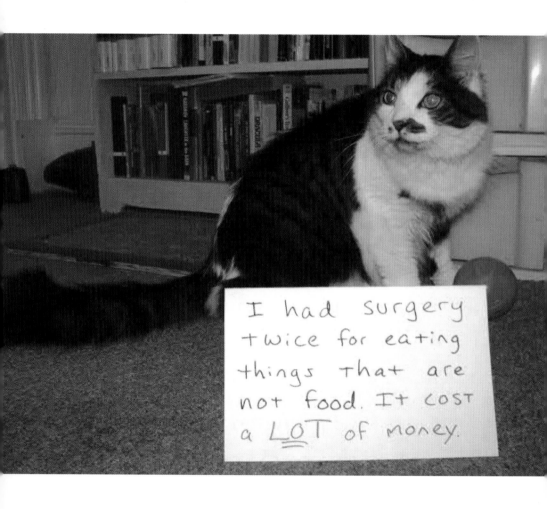

I had surgery twice for eating things that are not food. It cost a **LOT** of money.

MY AUNT TRUSTED ME
SO I WRIGGLED OUT
OF MY HARNESS AND
HID UNDER THE
DUMPSTER

MY DAD BOUGHT
ME A $20
SCRATCHING POST
AND I HAVEN'T USED IT
ONCE

(I prefer the couch and carpet)

I hide all day and convince
Mom I ran away.

LOST CAT

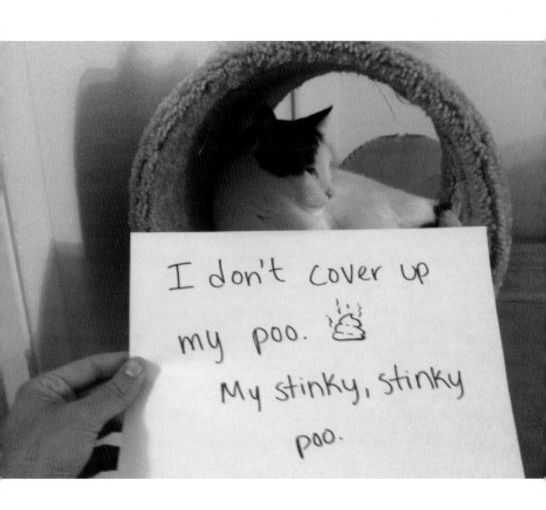

I CLIMB ONTO THE TABLE AND STEAL OTHER PEOPLE'S FOOD

NO SHAME!
Yes, this was CLEAN
laundry. Of course.

I DRINK
FROM
THE TOILET!
LIKE A DOG.

My sister brings in live rats ...

I THROW UP!!

I hate it when my mom is on one side of the closed door and I am on the other. So I tear the door to pieces.

IF I DON'T GET TO LAY ON MY PERSON FOR AT LEAST ONE HOUR EVERY NIGHT, I POOP ON THE MAT JUST OUTSIDE THE LITTER BOX.

125

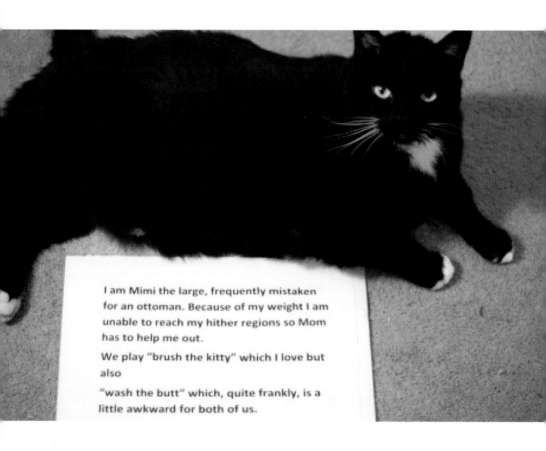

I am Mimi the large, frequently mistaken for an ottoman. Because of my weight I am unable to reach my hither regions so Mom has to help me out.

We play "brush the kitty" which I love but also

"wash the butt" which, quite frankly, is a little awkward for both of us.

I SCRATCHED MY MOMMY'S CHAIR, AND I FEEL NO REMORSE.

I EAT used
Q-Tips
from the
Trash

My Owner let me sleep on her bed. I thanked her by peeing on her shoe
— I'm fat and I SUCK

I stepped in my lady-human's mouth at 1:30 AM when she was sound asleep, after I'd clearly been in the cat box!!! And when she got up to Listerine like there was no tomorrow, I followed her and expected cuddles!

If someone stops petting me
and walks away, I chase
them down and bite
their feet!

I drag my human's stuffed animals down the stairs by the necks because i think I am a lion and then drown them in the dog's water bowl. Every. Single. Night. (I also meow really loud while doing it.)

Love – Foopa Toulouse

Last night after my mommy went to sleep, I played with her glasses so she had to spend over an hour looking for them this morning.

I'm not sorry. I'm too cute to stay mad at.

I tried to suffocate Mommy in her sleep this morning because she was not awake to feed me.

My Name is Matilda and I like to climb curtains at 3 a.m. !

I HUMP THE CAT

...AN[D] LIKE I[T]

151

I like to lie on my human's face while she is sleeping even though she is highly allergic to me, and to top it all off when she opens her eyes I stab her in them. I'm not even the slightest bit sorry.

Love, Jazzy

155

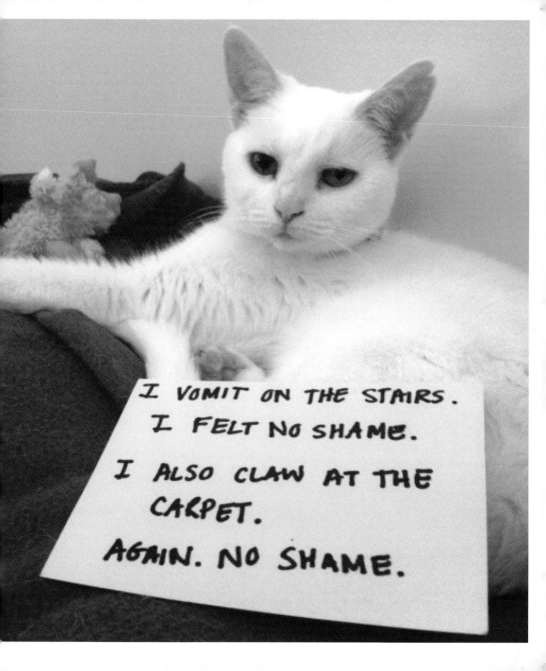

I don't think I can jump up here from the floor so I jump from the third stair and break this every time. My owners call me tubby.

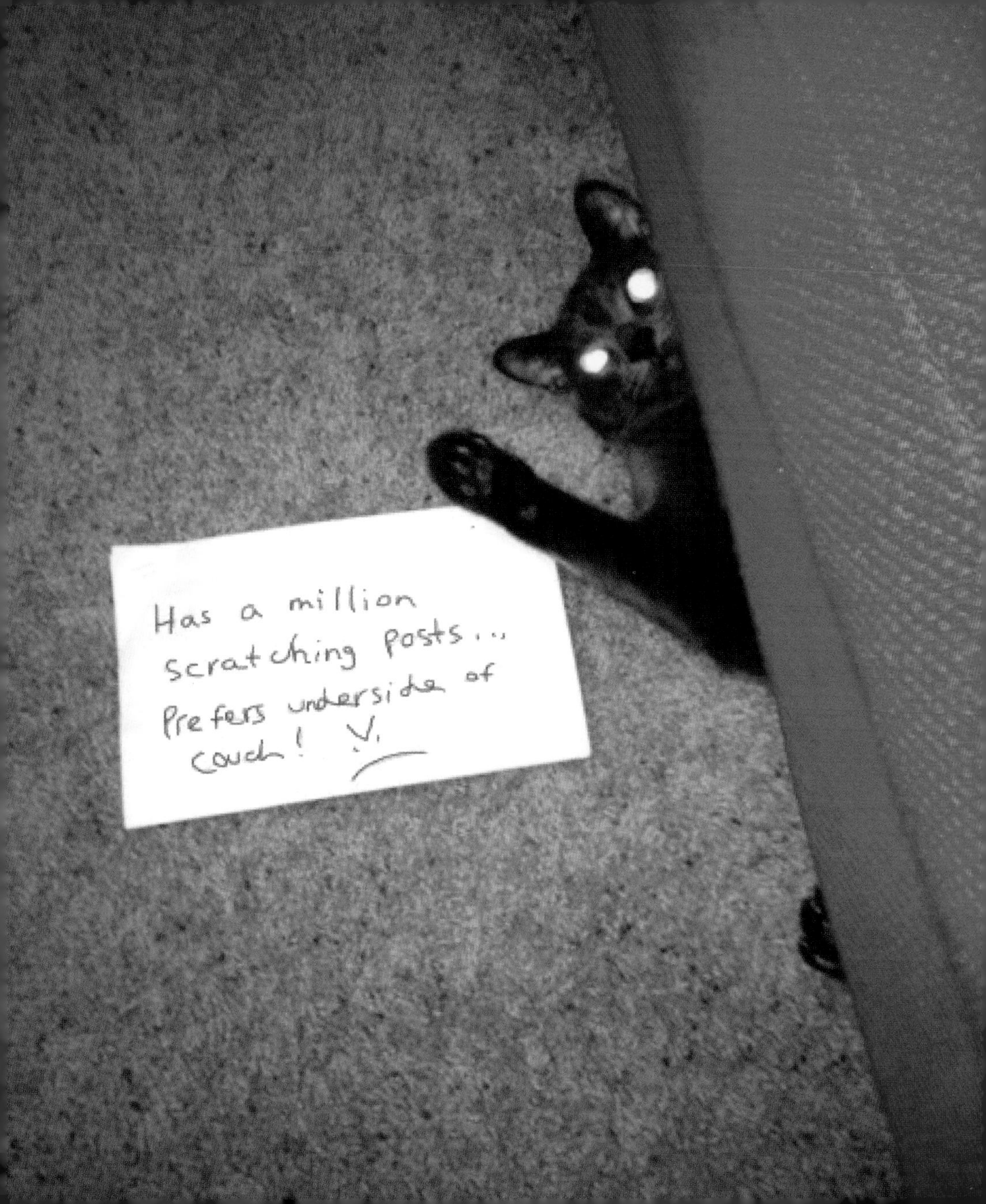
Has a million
scratching posts...
Prefers underside of
couch!

I somehow got
the lid off the urn

Then I SNEEZED
IN Grandma's ASHES!

I rack up $1,000 vet bills because I eat everything including hair ties and packing tape! I have no sympathy for my broke, college-aged human who rescued me from the pound!

— ♡ Milo

I like playing in the
dishwasher when Mommy
accidentally leaves it open.
— Wi-Fi

I was stuck in a
tree, 80 feet up, for 5
days in 95° heat. When
a lumberjack tried to
rescue me, I attacked
him.

Mom left her Snuggie behind the couch=new litter box.

Because of me, my parents will not be able to have a Christmas tree for many years. They are sure of that.

I head-butt people when they feed me so the food spills everywhere.

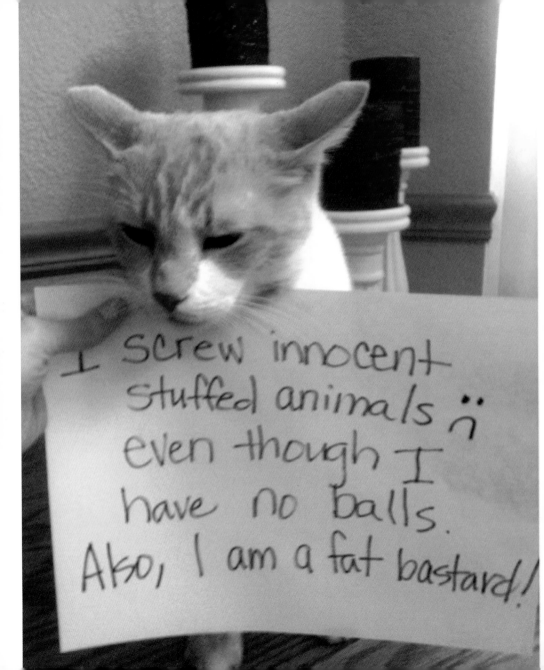

I must be the first to pull back the covers and sleep in the nicely made bed.

—Sterling

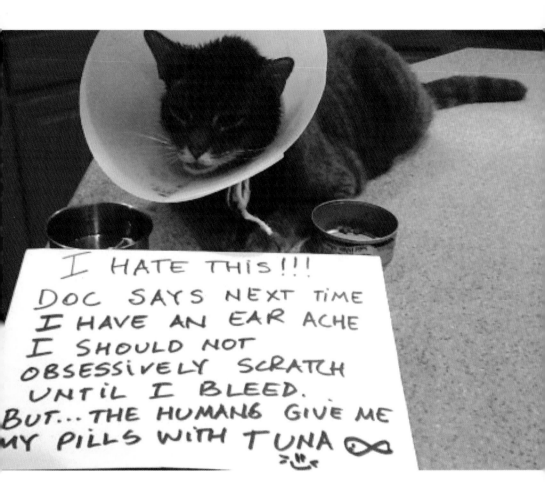

"I eat tape and plastic bags, then puke them up. I also terrorize my feline sibling and like to spill shit."

When I want to sit where my sister is sittin, I PUNCH HER IN THE <u>FACE</u>.

I Knocked a cactus over... directly into the dog's food bowls.

ACKNOWLEDGMENTS

First and foremost I'd like to take the time to thank the entire staff at Andrews McMeel Publishing, with a special thanks to Megan Sinclair and Alyce Leytham, who have put in so much of their time to make sure this book has become what I envisioned. I'd like to also thank Pascale Lemire (author of *Dog Shaming*) who inspired me to start *Cat Shaming* and who continues to inspire me. My family, thank you guys for teaching me to reach for my dreams and that hard work pays off. I'd like to thank my best friends Marbella Banuelos, Genesee Martinez, Betty Valdez, and Gigi, who have been the most supportive friends; thank you for being there with me and sticking with me through endless nights of trying to get the work done just right. And last but not least, every single one of my followers, all those who submitted every single one of these adorable, brave cats. To all those who have stuck around with the *Cat Shaming* blog: This has all been possible thanks to you. I will never be able to express my gratitude toward everyone involved with this book, but this book is a start.

CAT SHAMING

Andrews McMeel Publishing
a division of Andrews McMeel Universal
1130 Walnut Street, Kansas City, Missouri 64106

www.andrewsmcmeel.com

16 17 18 19 20 SBD 10 9 8 7 6 5 4 3 2 1

ISBN: 978-1-4494-7839-1

Library of Congress Control Number: 2015956866

Editor: Megan Sinclair
Art Director: Holly Ogden
Production Editor: Maureen Sullivan
Production Manager: Tamara Haus
Demand Planner: Sue Eikos

ATTENTION: SCHOOLS AND BUSINESSES

Andrews McMeel books are available at quantity discounts
with bulk purchase for educational, business, or sales
promotional use. For information, please e-mail the Andrews
McMeel Publishing Special Sales Department:
specialsales@amuniversal.com.